For Pearl and Isaac,
Your true love for life and dedication to each other brought us so much joy.

Dedication

This book is dedicated to Abbie Willmer and all her friends around the world who have dedicated their lives to working in developing countries to help make this a better planet for all of us. Abbie and her friends and colleagues gave up the comfort of their home country to help others thousands of miles away. She still meets yearly with her colleagues and friends, often traveling many miles to keep their relationships intact. We are forever grateful for their sense of mission and their humble humanity.

SNOWBALL AND ME

Written by **Nicholas E. Willmer-Shiles**
Inspired and Guided by **Sarah E. Willmer**
Art by **Gayle Kabaker**

1

A Unique Market and a Very Special Kitten

The sun rose above the distant mountains as I walked through the open-air market in the center of Tashkent, the capital of Uzbekistan. The unruly laughter of children playing with their toys spread along the market as I walked past the spice vendors, grateful for the shade of their rainbow-colored tents.

Smells of cumin, turmeric and saffron came up to greet me, drifting away from their peaks of reds and yellows like the sun rising before me. Past the spice mounds I found the grills covered with mounds of kebabs and the giant plates of spiced rice with beef called *plov*, enough to feed entire towns. A man in a purple and green coat called a *chapan* waved and offered me some lamb from his grill. I smiled but declined, I was not here to eat. I was here to find a friend.

I came to Uzbekistan from America to work, to help build a place for women like me, to help build communities, places to gather and talk with each other, places to learn about each other's lives, to learn about things that would help us thrive in a technological world. But everything was so different from America. We ate Uzbeki *lagman* instead of beef stew, we wore long and flowing kaftan dresses instead of jeans and t-shirts, children played with clay *babaychiki*, small and colorful ceramic dolls that were very different from plastic American toys. It often seemed to me that right was left and left was right. My cat Mika helped me through it all. She was there purring when my Uzbek lessons were going well, scratching when I moved her favorite pillow, snuggling up to me when I wore her favorite kaftan, even scolding me when I left the windows open in the rain. She helped me keep my lefts left, and my rights right. But now she was gone. Escaping one night to hunt mice through the bushes, Mika lost her way and it had been a long time since I had seen my best friend.

Beyond the grills now, I could see the cages and kennels of the animal breeders stacked neatly between huge patterned curtains. The sun's rays shifted back and forth between them as they swayed in the gentle breeze, as if they were beckoning me closer. I walked slowly towards them, suddenly feeling more than a little nervous. Mika could never be replaced, but would I even be able to find another companion for my work and travels? Would any of the cats even like me? Despite my fears I approached the stacks of cages; I so very much needed a friend and if I didn't even look how could I be sure my companion wasn't here? Rounding a corner I saw and felt the peaceful gaze of dozens of animals on my face. Feeling so at peace, as if I had entered a sort of heaven, the gazes of the cats and dogs of all types told me I would be okay, that everything would be okay. In that moment I knew I would find my companion here.

2

Snowball and Caissa Meet: The Beginning of a Bond

With that assurance, I slowed down to look at all of the wonderful pets that were on display. I saw rows of dogs with ears perked up over friendly following eyes.

I saw countless cats carefully cleaning their gleaming coats or stretching out, limbs spread wide, lazily collecting the rays of the afternoon sun. As I rounded a corner I suddenly stopped still. A pair of large golden eyes stared at me curiously, expectantly, and right away I knew. There he was in pristine white fur, slowly waving his tail back and forth as if to tell me, "Here I am, come collect me; I've been waiting for you!"

"Aren't you wonderful," I whispered to the kitten now firmly nestled in my arms. "What will you be called?" He responded with a purr, closed his eyes and settled deeply into the crook of my elbow. "I think you will be called *Tabi Barfi*." The name meant Snowball in Uzbek and I don't think there was a more perfect name for him in the world. He was as white as fresh snow after a winter storm.

The owner of the stall informed me that Snowball was a purebred Persian, a very desirable breed. I thought that was nice but I didn't care too much about any of that. I just knew that when I locked eyes with him, it was love at first sight. With Snowball in my arms the rest of my anxiety melted away. The insecurity that had lingered with me all day was gone. I had found my partner, and as I watched the sun turn into a deep amber behind the mountains, I knew it was time to head home.

3

Snowball's New Home: Off to Qarshi

The next morning, I started to pack up all my things to get ready for the train ride back to Qarshi, the city in the South of Uzbekistan where I was living and working. As I packed, Snowball was very curious about all my embroidered kaftans and my jewelry. He loved playing with the necklaces and bracelets and wrapping himself in whatever cloth he found available. As disruptive as he was being, I couldn't help but smile.

His playfulness was an affirmation of our new bond and my heart swelled with joy, all of the contentment and peace that I had felt in the market yesterday came flooding back to me now. Eventually I was able to wrangle my clothes away from him and roll everything up neatly into my bag. As we were about to leave, I realized I had not brought anything for Snowball to travel in! However, as I looked around for a blanket, or something to wrap him in, Snowball jumped right on top of the open bag and looked at me expectantly, as if saying, "Okay, I'm ready to go now!" I gave him a kiss on the top of his head and zipped up three quarters of the bag so he could keep his head poked out to examine his surroundings. And with that we were off for the train.

I was nervous that Snowball would become anxious surrounded by all the strange sounds of the people traveling and the strange scenery, and by the smell of coffees and beers that filled the car. Of course, he was perfectly fine. He seemed to enjoy the sound of mothers scolding their children and the slap of cards hitting the fold-out tables. While looking through the windows at the lush trees and the purple and blue rocks of mountains passing by, he looked up at me and meowed as his eyes narrowed slightly. "Of course! You're a traveling boy; you must be very hungry." I scolded myself as I reached into my shoulder bag and pulled out a tin of wet food. He sniffed the spoon I offered him to make sure it was acceptable, then he went at it with small, precise licks. After finishing the can, he took another long look at the afternoon sunlight before curling up on my tunics and falling asleep.

At the next stop we were given some time to get off the train to stretch our legs. I took Snowball to a *choyxana*, an Uzbek teahouse, and as I was enjoying my tea a young woman sat down near us. When she saw Snowball, she looked a little sad. She looked back at me and starting speaking in Uzbek. "That is a beautiful cat, I used to have a Persian just like it but I had to leave her behind when I moved to

Qarshi with my family." A little confused, I asked her, "Why would you have to do that?" "You see," she said, "Persian cats are famous for their unique flat, squished nose, which makes it more difficult for them to breathe when the air is thinner. This can make flying very dangerous for them and many airlines do not want to deal with these added risks. Our family could not find a way to bring him on the plane with us from Poland so I had to say goodbye to my little Baba." She looked at Snowball longingly, seeing the memory of her poor Baba on his bright white fur. Her story saddened and worried me; my work required me to move every two years and I only had a few months left in Qarshi before I would be given a new assignment. I looked down at my little Snowball sleeping so peacefully on his blanket and in that moment I knew I would find a way to keep my furry companion, no matter what.

Snowball's New Friend, Mika's Return

Snowball made himself quite at home upon arrival at my house in Qarshi. Spending his time pawing at the embroidered rugs, sniffing the wood of the detailed carvings of the chest of drawers and cabinets, rolling around on the aged but still magnificently velvet couch. Eventually he claimed a cushion on the end of the couch as his own. The colors of the cushion were faded, its stitching frayed, and some of its stuffing could be seen poking out of one end.

But when he curled up his paws and looked at me before going to sleep, I knew he loved that cushion and that he loved me. When he was not taking his naps on the couch, my Snowball was inspecting the baroque walls of the house, painted with Slavic patterns from the 1600s, or exploring the courtyard, smelling the figs and apricots that hung high in their trees above his path.

I returned to work with the women of Qarshi with Snowball now as my partner. He loved when I had my lessons in Uzbek, curling up in my lap to listen to me reciting vocabulary and verbs, purring contentedly when I got my words right and always meowing goodbye at my teacher when she left. It was a great comfort to know that he was guarding my house when I was out working. When I lived in Qarshi, I traveled to rural areas to help women learn how to develop and support business practices for their local trades. We worked together to form groups of women in the same neighborhoods who could get together and apply for loans to help them run businesses like local tea houses, craft shops, and small farms. I told everyone in my community of my little prince Snowball and our house soon became a favorite meeting place. These were my favorite days, when we would gather as women and share the stories of our lives with one another, laughing and learning from each other's joys and experiences, while my little Snowball wound around the living room greeting everyone he could. He loved the attention from my visitors and the delicious treats they brought him. He would walk between our legs as we talked about life and family. We learned about each other's fathers, mothers, brothers and sisters, their accomplishments and troubles, and we always spoke about how women are the necessary backbone of a rich and vibrant society and how we must work with each other, helping each other to create welcoming spaces where all women can feel free to express themselves and feel loved.

As the months passed in Qarshi, I continued my work with the women of Uzbekistan and Snowball grew into a fine young cat. He always seemed at peace, greeting my friends with gentle meows and always finding a perfectly amber ray of sun for cat naps. Every night he pawed at the fringed blanket at the edge of my bed before hopping up and snuggling into my side to sleep for the night.

One day, however, something amazing happened. I was just returning to Qarshi from Beshchasma, a town nearby where I had been working with local farmers. As I was settling in for the night, a man came to my door saying he had found a lost cat and after asking around, he was told that it used to live at my address. I opened the door fully and saw my Mika nestled in his arms! For a moment I didn't believe what I was seeing. It had been so long since I'd lost Mika, I had always hoped that she would be okay out on her own, but over time I had come to accept that I would probably never see her again. I wondered how he had found her, but I did not question it when he asked for a small "finder's fee" to take her back. I cried and cried holding her in my arms, so thankful to have her back. It was a wonderful feeling, knowing our little family was whole and growing, much like the community of women who brought me so much joy.

The next morning Mika and Snowball met for the first time. She was very excited, sniffing his fur and rolling around trying to play with him, but Snowball wasn't interested in playing. He gave Mika a sideways look and sauntered off to his favorite cushion for a nap. For awhile, Snowball was quite annoyed by Mika—Mika thought sunbathing on a cushion was all well and good, but wanted Snowball to do more than just lie around all day, every day. She jumped and ran around and always seemed to be disturbing his long and frequent naps. Soon, though, Snowball grew to like Mika and her antics. The joy and excitement Mika brought to the sunlit rugs and pillows in Qarshi was just what Snowball needed. I watched from the open doors of my study while Mika nipped at Snowball's tail until he joined in the fun, my heart feeling very full indeed as our little family grew closer together with each passing day.

5

A New Journey Begins, Mongolia Awaits

Months passed peacefully like this in Qarshi and I had almost forgotten about what the young woman on the train had said to me, about how very difficult it was to travel with Persian cats. Then one day I got a phone call from the United Nations.

I was being offered a job with the United Nations Volunteers, an organization that contracted people from all over the world to do social work. I was to move from Uzbekistan to Ulaanbaatar, the capital of Mongolia. I wanted to be excited to live and work in a new country, learn a new language and eat new food, but all I could think about now was how would I travel with Snowball? Would I be able to find an airline that would take him? Would he be safe if I did? Before I could find that out, Snowball and Mika would need to get their vaccines to make sure they would not bring any diseases to their new home of Mongolia.

At the hospital for her shots, Mika was very nervous. Her black hair stood straight up as if she had just been shocked and she arched her back when the doctor came close. Snowball, on the other hand, was very calm, simply batting his tail and looking around, wondering when he could get back to his napping. He did not growl or hiss when it was his time to receive his shot; he simply looked at the doctor as if to say, "Are you finished yet? I have important things to attend to!" After two successful vaccine treatments we all made our way to the local government travel office where Snowball and Mika were given their very own passports! The documents were very official, with handsome pictures in the corner and all the information they would need for the journey to Mongolia.

7

A Growing Family in Mongolia

Our new home in Ulaanbaatar was on a quiet tree-lined street away from the hustle of the city center. I especially loved it in the late afternoon when the sun shone through the trees and mosaics of light and shadow rested on the sidewalks. It was in our Mongolian home that Snowball and Mika became a kitty family. They had three kittens, two of them looked exactly like Mika and the third took after Snowball; he had golden eyes but his fur was pure black. I named him Midnight.

The only problem was that Korean Air would only allow me to travel with one companion by my side, the other would have to go in a special hold for traveling pets. I had Mika's old cage. However, when it was time to leave I could not for the life of me find a suitable traveling compartment for Snowball! I looked all over but had to make due with a large blue plastic basket, much like the ones that people used to carry all sorts of wares at the Tashkent Market. I packed the basket with blankets and a large pillow, wondering if my little prince would be nervous about leaving our home and flying around the world, but Snowball settled in easily to his traveling basket. At the airport Mika wiggled in circles in her cage and looked from side to side nervously, but Snowball hardly made a sound except to clean a bit of hair off of his paw. He looked up at me expectantly, ready to begin our new life in Ulaanbaatar. When it came time to board the plane I was forced to make the decision on who would be traveling next to me. Mika was so afraid and nervous of all the sights and sounds that I knew she would have to travel next to me. I worried about Snowball, my little prince, but when I remembered seeing him curled up and sleeping so peacefully in his basket, I knew he wouldn't even have noticed the sounds of the airplane or the many bumps and shakes when we passed through blowing winds. What was on his mind was the nice meal and cool shade that awaited him in his new home in Mongolia.

The Journey to Mongolia.

6

A Cat, A Basket, and an Airplane

Everyone was ready for the journey to Mongolia but the only airline I could find that would possibly let me travel with Snowball was Korean Air. This meant I had to fly to Seoul, South Korea before we could move on to Mongolia.

Mika, always the protective mother, watched closely as the kittens rolled and jumped about the house, always nipping and pawing at each other playfully. I felt safe knowing she was watching while I worked on my lessons in Mongolian, always with Snowball at my side, licking at his treats and meowing in approval at my slow, but steady progress.

I very much enjoyed my time in Mongolia. The work that had been assigned to me by the United Nations was quite different from my work in Uzbekistan. In Mongolia I worked with youth groups to spread knowledge about medical awareness and prevention of diseases. Whether you are from Mongolia or Uzbekistan, New York or Paris, there are many things that we as humans must deal with all over the world, regardless of race or nationality, and knowing that I was helping to educate the next generation on universal medical issues gave me a strong sense of connection to my new home. I became close friends with many of the people I worked with, and we often joked and laughed as we ate Mongolian dumplings and cheese curds, called *Buuz* and *Aaruul*. Mongolian is such a powerful language. To me it felt and sounded like a spell, mystical and ancient. I often spoke to Snowball in Mongolian as he sat purring on my lap after his children had gone to sleep. Although Ulaanbaatar was quite a bit larger than Qarshi, and Snowball did not have his fruit trees to explore, he felt quite comfortable in our apartment up in the sky. When I had friends over, he loved to dart between our legs before leaping to his place beside me, meowing ever so politely for the treats he so well deserved. During this time Snowball grew into a fine father, calm, protective and kind to his brood, always making sure the kittens were clean and well rested, letting them sleep, curled up and comfy resting against his back as he surveyed the drifting clouds and the buildings below us from his favorite window in my bedroom. He kept an especially close eye on Midnight, who was the smallest of the bunch, making sure he was never too far out of sight.

Eventually I knew my time in Mongolia would come to an end. The day came when the United Nations called to give me my new assignment: Kabul, Afghanistan. I was ready for our new adventure but leaving felt bittersweet. I would miss my Mongolian friends dearly but when I told Snowball the news of our move, his ears perked up and he meowed at me in excitement as if to say, "Don't worry, I'll be there to help, and of course everyone will love me so you'll make lots of friends!" Before leaving I had to find homes for Snowball and Mika's children; I simply could not travel with so many cats. Mika was very attached to her other kittens and fortunately I was able to find them a loving home with one of my neighbors in our apartment building. Still, I couldn't bring myself to separate Snowball and Midnight so I decided they both would come with me to Afghanistan.

S

A Vacation in the Sun Before a Long Journey

Before moving on to Kabul, I needed to return to the United States to renew my visa. I thought this might be a perfect time to introduce Snowball and his son to my own family, and with that we set off for Los Angeles. Luckily this time we were all able to travel together, and in California Snowball and Midnight got many tasty treats of fish and chicken at my brother's house.

While I spent time with my family, Snowball and Midnight enjoyed bathing in the warm glow of the Southern California sun, stretching out under the shade of the palm trees. They had many, good long cat naps in Los Angeles and Snowball dreamed of plush Afghani cushions for sitting, silky blankets for kneading, and new friends for himself and Midnight. After a few weeks of some much-needed rest and relaxation, it was time for us to move on to Kabul.

Our travels to Afghanistan turned out to be quite the adventure, one I would never forget. I was on a strict deadline to begin my work in Afghanistan. But as I searched for flights to take my traveling family across the globe, my conversation with the woman at the teahouse swirled around inside my head. Sadly, I could not find an airline that would allow me to travel straight to Afghanistan with Snowball. His squished nose and breathing issues were simply too much of a risk to fly all the way from California to Central Asia. The only solution I could find was for Snowball to travel on a different airline to Frankfurt, Germany, and then on to Dubai where I could go collect him and take him to our new home in Afghanistan. As I made the plans, I was overwhelmed with thoughts of my friend from the teahouse back in Uzbekistan. How longingly she had looked at Snowball, and I could feel the sadness in her voice as she told me of leaving behind her little Baba. Although I knew from our trip to Mongolia that Snowball would not mind flying, the idea of him traveling on a completely different plane made me feel very unsettled. Who knew what could happen to a cat traveling alone on some foreign airline without his closest friend alongside? The night before our journey, I could barely sleep, as thoughts of everything going wrong raced around my mind. As if he could read my mind at that troubled moment, Snowball walked into my room and hopped up in my arms, hugging me with his paws and purring softly as if to say, "Everything is going to be okay."

The morning of our journey came and I told myself that if Snowball wasn't nervous, why should I be? Snowball, being the cool cat that he was, calmly curled up onto his little cushion in the carrier and went to sleep. Seeing my Snowball so calm and peaceful finally made me feel okay about our journey and we headed off to the airport. There, I checked Snowball in for his flight, and then Midnight and I boarded ours. The plane ride was very long but I was glad to have Midnight there for company, and by the time we landed in Dubai I was very excited to collect my Snowball and set off for our new adventure together in Afghanistan. But then it happened...

At the airline's collection desk, I gave the attendant my collection papers for Snowball and his itinerary. As soon as she began searching his information in her computer, I knew something was wrong. Her brow furrowed and she kept typing and typing but didn't look up. Finally, she told me that there had been a problem with Snowball's schedule and that he was still back in Frankfurt! "Oh no, no no no..." What did this mean, who would take care of him? Where would he stay? What was I to do without my best friend? What was he to do without me? Would he ever make it to Dubai? Worse yet, I couldn't stay in Dubai, I had to go on to Kabul to begin my new position. My body ached with worry!

Once I got to Kabul I was worried sick and I still had heard nothing about my Snowball. For a whole week I could barely sleep. What if Snowball's documents were never approved? What if his papers with his name on it were lost and no one knew where he belonged? How was he being treated? No one at the airport knew what he liked or how to make him comfortable. Would he miss Midnight and be sad and lonely the whole time? With my heart in my throat, I waited every day with the phone beside me for news about my little prince.

10

Home at last, Caissa, Snowball, and Midnight Make it to Afghanistan

As soon as I opened the door, Snowball leapt into my arms, his eyes gleaming and his many meows saying, “Oh my goodness, you would not believe the adventure I just had! I met all these strange people but they were all so nice to me! I hope you’ve been taking good care of Midnight!” “Oh, I’m so glad you’re okay,” I told him, with my mouth pressed into his fur. “I don’t know what I would do without you in our new home!” And with that we boarded our flight to Kabul, eager to reunite our family.

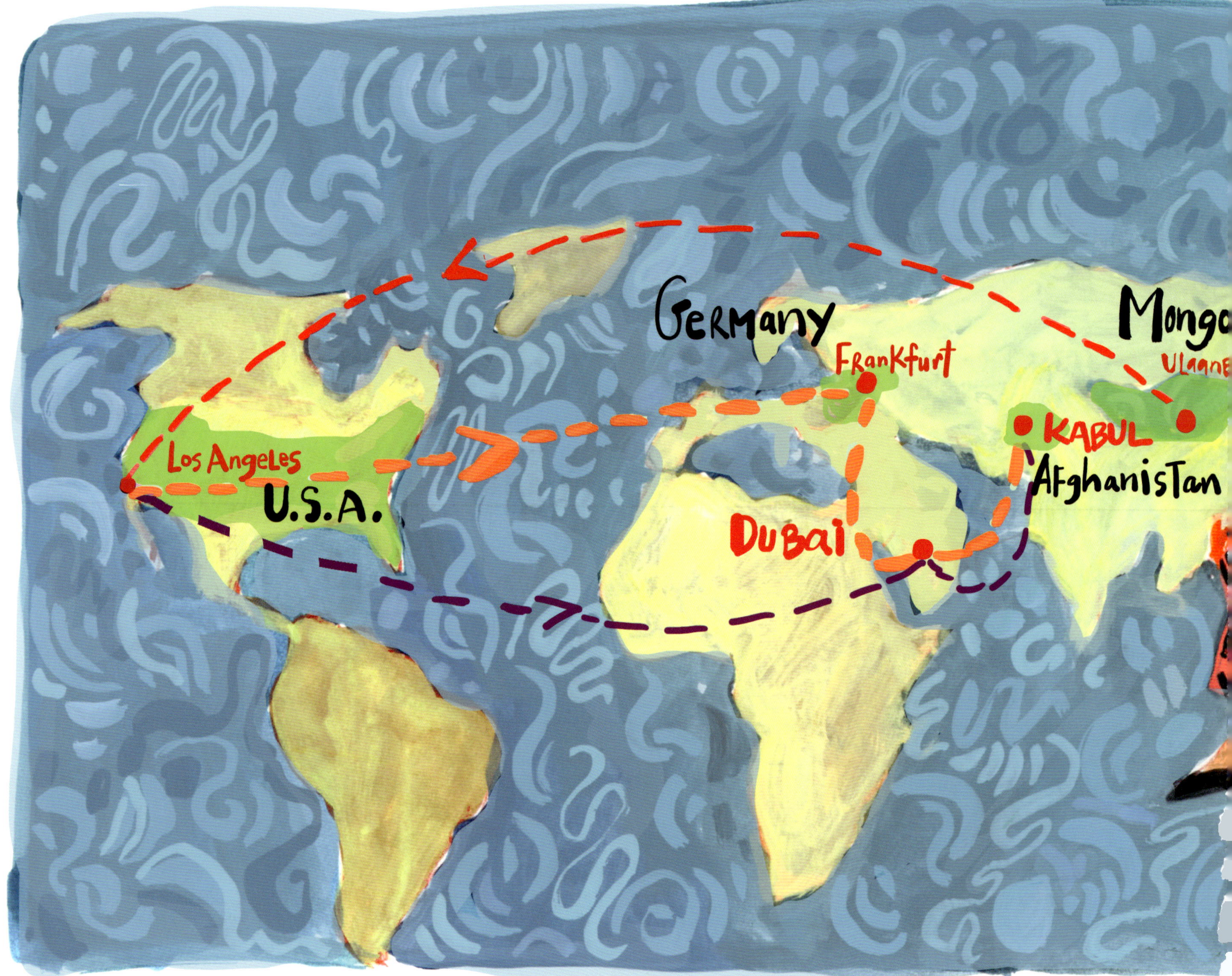

Germany
Frankfurt
Los Angeles
U.S.A.
Dubai
KABUL
Afghanistan

He was so handsome and sweet that everyone at the airport wanted to take turns caring for him. Every day he had been given the best food and lots of attention, and his days in Germany were filled with tuna and fresh milk and all the massages and scratches any cat could ever want. “Of course!” I thought to myself. “How could he not be loved, and how could I have worried that he would not be treated like a king?”

I left Midnight with my housemate and flew back to Dubai the very next day to collect my Snowball. When I arrived at the collection desk, I couldn’t spot his familiar carrier. The man at the counter then pointed to a very fancy travel carrier. It turned out that Snowball was so loved by the people at the Frankfurt airport that the airline had bought him a brand-new traveling home, with a new deep red embroidered cushion, fit for a king!

Snowball + Caissa Fly to LA
Caissa’s Flight to Kabul
Snowball’s Flight to Kabul

A family visit and on to Afghanistan.

9

Snowball the Unexpected Celebrity

After what seemed like ages, I finally received the call I had prayed for: Snowball was on his way to Dubai! What's more, the woman who called me said that Snowball had turned into a huge celebrity in the Frankfurt airport! She went on and on about how well-behaved and regal Snowball was, and how handsome he was, with his pure white fur and his golden eyes!

When we finally reached our house in Kabul, Snowball jumped down and was promptly greeted by Midnight, who swiftly pounced on him and began nipping at his tail. Snowball was delighted to see his son again and the two played and wrestled for a long time. After their playful reunion, Snowball got up to make his own personal inspection. For him, our new home seemed like a palace. Rugs of every color and pattern covered the floors from wall to wall, and tapestries made of rare and beautiful threads hung across the couches and beds. Soon he loved pawing at the bits of string hanging off the rugs and squeezing between the cushions for a little bit of privacy after a meal. For him, the wood of the chairs was worn and warm, perfect for curling up in the afternoon rays of the Afghan sun.

Snowball's favorite place was the garden. There were so many trees and vines and vibrant flowers blooming at every turn; it was his own personal forest. Sometimes when my guests were too loud, or he just wanted to be alone, Snowball tucked himself into a quiet corner of the garden, where, undisturbed, he could watch the people in the house and follow the birds up in the treetops.

My work in Afghanistan was similar to my work in Uzbekistan. In Kabul my colleagues and I helped set up training centers for women to manage the economics of different trades. Through this training, women learned how to make money in local activities like computer repair, jewelry making, and selling produce. These were skills that would help them enrich their lives and those of their families. Unlike in Uzbekistan and Mongolia, the other UN workers and I had to live in a special compound together in Kabul. This was quite a change for me, not having the same freedom to explore and find new things. Now I was even more grateful for my Snowball, especially after our unexpected adventure. His warm and peaceful presence brought me all the joy and confidence in the world.

After all of Snowball's globe-trotting adventures, and the joys of raising his family, Kabul was the perfect place for him to settle in. Together with Midnight, now fully grown, Snowball lived happily with many treats and naps, always with me and Midnight right by his side. By the end, Snowball was much more than a cat to me. He represented all of my experiences moving through the world: the people I met, the relationships I built, the communities I joined and helped create—Snowball was a cherished part of all of it. By his presence alone, he reminded me of the toughness and resilience of the women I had the honor of working with, of their dedication to their friends and family, and their ability to support and lift up those around them. Someday I would have to leave Afghanistan, to travel somewhere new to continue my work. But I knew that after all we had been through together, Snowball would always be by my side, the best companion anyone could ever have.

A Final Word, From Sarah Willmer

The realization that Snowball's story would make a wonderful children's book came to me when catching up with my sister Abbie during one of her bi-yearly visits from her work overseas. Abbie always came home from far off lands like Tanzania, Ghana and the Philippines with tales of her volunteer work helping the people of these countries to utilize local resources and trades to create woman-owned micro-businesses. Her work during these early years of her career was as a volunteer with the U.S. Peace Corps, VSO (Volunteer Service Overseas-the British organization similar to our Peace Corps), NGO's (Non-Government Organizations), and United Nations Volunteers.

During this time, Abbie helped local women develop their skills in textiles, crafts or animal husbandry—skills they had been taught by their mothers and fathers—and turned them into sources of sustainable income and effective ways to provide for their families in a modern globalized world. This was exciting and very important work, and Abbie made lifelong friendships with people from all over the world. Her passion for helping others was truly inspiring for everyone who knew her. With every story my sister told me, the more convinced I became that we needed to share her story with a wider audience.

The result was a true family endeavor. Our father was a geographer and our mother was a writer and someone who celebrated the richness of all cultures. So it was only natural for us to celebrate Abbie's love for Snowball and other animals with stories describing the unique experiences she had working with women in different parts of the world. As this became a family project, it was only natural for me to ask my son Nick to write the story. I am an architect and not the writer that he is. Because our mother was a prolific writer, attuned to other cultures, we decided to use her pen name, Caissa, as Abbie's name in the telling of her story. At its core, then, *Snowball and Me* is based on true events, and we hope that Abbie's adventures and her caring spirit will touch hearts here and all around the world.

SNOWBALL AND ME

First Edition 2025

Published by Val de Grâce Books, Napa, California

ISBN 979-8-9858787-4-5

Library of Congress Control Number: 2024915601

Design by Connie Hwang Design

Printed by Artron Art Printing (HK) Ltd through Crash Paper